W9-AGE-746

ROCKS AND MINERALS

FROM THIS EARTH

William Russell

The Rourke Corporation, Inc.
Vero Beach, Florida 32964

PHOTO CREDITS:
All photos© William Russell except p.15, courtesy U.S. Geological
Survey

Library of Congress Cataloging-in-Publication Data

Russell, William, 1942–
    Rocks and minerals / by William Russell.
        p. cm. — (From this earth)
    Includes index
    ISBN 0-86593-362-6
    1. Rocks—Juvenile literature. 2. Minerals—Juvenile literature.
[1. Rocks. 2. Minerals.]
I. Title II. Series.
QE432.2.R87 1994
552—dc20
                                                    94–507
                                                    CIP
                                                    AC

Printed in the USA

TABLE OF CONTENTS

MINERALS

The Earth is wrapped in a hard crust. That crust is made of many different solid materials called minerals. Minerals are not living, nor were they ever living.

Altogether there are about 3,000 different kinds of minerals. Only about 100 of them are plentiful, like halite, which we know better as table salt.

A mineral is sometimes difficult to tell apart from another mineral or other natural material. Scientists can tell minerals apart with laboratory equipment.

Inside a Florida cave, the mineral calcite forms stone "icicles"

HOW MINERALS LOOK

Different minerals exist in a variety of shapes, colors and forms. They can be stringy, lumpy, rough, smooth, fuzzy, bright, dull, soft or hard.

Most of the minerals that we use in our daily lives have been processed, or changed. They don't usually look, or feel, much like they did in nature.

The hard mineral fluorite, for example, can be processed into fluoride. Fluoride is added to some toothpastes.

One form or another of the mineral fluorite is used in the making of aluminum and toothpaste

MINERALS WE KNOW BEST

The mineral graphite is the "lead" in pencils. Calcite is used in baking soda. Mineral stones, such as diamonds and rubies, are polished, cut and used for jewelry.

Fluoride—from fluorite—helps prevent tooth decay. Sulphur, which has a "rotten egg" smell, is commonly used in medicines.

Copper is an important metal mineral used in wires and pipes

ROCKS

Certain types of minerals and combinations of minerals are called rocks. Most rock material is underground. Hot, liquid rock lies deep underground. It is sometimes pushed upward in **volcanoes**. Rocks on or near the Earth's surface are usually hard, quite solid and heavy.

The Earth has been making rocks for millions of years. Scientists who study rocks—**geologists**—have found rocks they believe to be about 3 billion years old.

Old lava rock field at Craters of the Moon National Monument in Idaho

Gold, amethyst and other minerals are crafted into a castle and courtyard at the Lazzadro Museum of Lapidary Arts in Elmhurst, Illinois

ROCKS FROM VOLCANOES

Geologists lump rocks into three major groups. How a rock was formed decides to which group it belongs.

Rocks that begin as hot liquid deep in the Earth are called **igneous** rocks. Sometimes liquid rock—**lava**—"escapes" through volcanoes.

Lava cools and hardens on the Earth's surface. Lava is the best known type of igneous rock.

A fiery fountain of lava erupts from Paricutin volcano in Mexico

ROCKS THAT "CHANGE"

Heat and pressure are powerful forces at work below the Earth's surface. Over millions of years, these forces and others shape and change rocks.

Metamorphic rocks are the kinds that have undergone a change deep in the Earth. Metamorphic rocks are lifted to the Earth's surface by earthquakes and mountains.

Marble and slate are common metamorphic rocks.

16 *Students examine metamorphic and igneous rocks*

WEATHERING

The forces of nature wear away rocks and earth. One of the great forces is weather. Rain, wind, heat, cold and wind-driven dirt slowly change large rocks into smaller rocks. Over long periods, weather cracks, chips, flakes and crumbles rocks. As rocks **weather**, or wear away, the pieces become smaller still—rock powder.

Huge rivers of ice called **glaciers** and tiny plantlike growths of **lichen** weather rocks, too.

Rain, wind and rivers have weathered sedimentary rock layers into "badlands" at Badlands National Park, South Dakota

ROCKS FROM POWDER

Streams and rivers carry some of the rock powder, called **sediment**, to the sea. Layer after layer of rock powder weighs upon the layers below it.

Over millions of years, the weight of water and sediment squeezes older layers of sediment into solid, sedimentary rock.

Sedimentary rock reaches the Earth's surface through earthquakes or through weathering. Sandstone is a common sedimentary rock.

Sandstone cliffs, stained by the mineral iron oxide, overlook the Belle Fourche River in Wyoming

STUDYING ROCKS AND MINERALS

The work of geologists helps people to find important rocks and minerals, such as marble, slate, copper, salt and uranium.

Geologists also help people learn more about things of which the Earth is made.

Among other things, geologists study earthquakes and volcanoes. Their studies help people to know when earthquakes and volcanoes might happen and where they might happen.

Glossary

geologist (gee AHL uh gist) — scientist who studies rocks, minerals, earthquakes, volcanoes and land forms

glacier (GLAY shur) — a massive river of ice

igneous (IG nee us) — having to do with fire, as in "rocks of fire"—igneous rocks

lava (LAH vuh) — melted rock that pours out of a volcano and later hardens

lichen (LIE kin) — a plantlike growth that commonly grows on rocks and trees

metamorphic (met uh MOR fihk) — referring to change, as in rocks that change

sediment (SEHD uh ment) — dirt or sand; particles of dirt and sand

volcano (vahl KAY no) — an opening in the Earth and the mountain of rock that forms around it from forces underground

weather (WEH thur) — to wear away rocks and soil by rain, wind, cold, heat and snow

INDEX